How to Write and Self-Publish Your Book for FREE with Amazon's KDP

Leslie's Lane Presents………………..

How to Write and Self-Publish Your Book for FREE with Amazon's KDP

*An Easy Way to Complete Your Manuscript
in Seven Stress-Free Steps*

Leslie E. Royal

Volume III of The Leslie's Lane Series

While permission has been granted by Kindle Direct Publishing (KDP) to use its name and that of Amazon, the companies have not endorsed this book.

Contents

*Don't doubt another person's dream. Support it. Remember, the
dream is for the eyes of the DREAMER and The CREATOR.*
Donna London

Introduction

Greetings Beautiful Friends!

How are you? I trust that you are having a great day! Congrats to you!
I say that because you've just taken one of the first steps to becoming
an author!!!!! AWESOME! I'm really excited for you! You're ready
to share your gift of writing with the world! It's a wonderful feeling,
isn't it?
I know that feeling! I felt that way in the Spring of 2016 as I sat down
to begin writing my first book. After 20 years of writing
professionally for several international publications, my writing came
full circle in the completion of *Leslie's Lane The Book!* Since
then…… well……. Actually….. before then ………. many people
shared that they wanted to write a book and needed information on
how to do so. Moreover, others shared they have written their novel,
autobiography or other book of their choice and needed to know how
to publish it.
To both queries, I would respond, "Well, I don't know. But I will find
out." It is my pleasure to share what I have learned about how to write
and publish your book – and for FREE! This user-friendly, easy to
read book will include my posing questions to prompt you to respond
and spur you to immediate action TODAY! All the best and I look
forward to seeing your book on newsstands, in bookstores and on
websites in the very near future!

Sincerely,

Leslie

This Book is Dedicated to My Beautiful Mother!
"All Hail The Queen!"

I dedicate this book to my beautiful mother – Mrs. Lizzie M. Dukes Guess. You are such an inspiration to me! You have always taught me that anything worth doing is worth doing exceptionally well! And as a young girl, you told me to "Reach for the moon. If you miss, you will still land among the stars!" I thank you for that! I work hard every day – just to make you proud of me! I love you dearly and thank God for you!

"Time to Celebrate Mama"

Chapter 1

Step One – Utilize The 5 W's (and sometimes HOW)

"What are the top five steps I should take in beginning to write my first book?" Dr. Davine S. Ricks

Okay. You're on Leslie's Line. Let's talk! We can take a "5-pronged plus 1" approach to Step One. In my journalism classes in middle and high school, my teachers always insisted that an article contain: who, what, when, where, why, and sometimes how. To get started, can we apply "The 5 W's and How" thought process as you begin writing your book? If you run out of space in the blanks of this book, feel free to use a notepad or loose leaf paper.

Why:
Why would you like to write a book?

_____
_____
_____
_____
_____
_____
_____

What:
What is your book about?

_____
_____
_____
_____
_____
_____
_____
_____

When:
When do you plan to write your book?

_____

_____

_____

_____

_____

Who:
Who is your target audience?

_____

_____

_____

_____

_____

Where:
Where can you go to relax and feel comfortable as you write your awesome book?

_____

_____

_____

_____

_____

How:
How are you going to focus and commit to beginning and ending the writing of your book in a timely manner? (I say this because it is easy to get distracted and procrastinate.)

_____

_____

_____

_____

_____

_____
_____
_____
_____

Next………. What Is Your Working Title?

No worries if you have not settled on the name of your book just yet. Can you just give it a working title for now?

_____
_____
_____
_____
_____

Miscellaneous Notes………

_____
_____
_____
_____
_____
_____
_____
_____
_____
_____
_____
_____
_____
_____
_____
_____
_____
_____
_____

Now that you have written down what your book is about, think about what you want to include in your book. You can even place it in bullet or list form.

Let's Try This………..
Can you start jotting down subjects or topics that you would like to see in your book? Don't worry if you don't know precisely what they will be. Just begin to list whatever topics come to mind below. I knew exactly what I wanted to include in *Leslie's Lane The Book!* The ten sub-topics that I brainstormed in my list turned out to be the ten chapters in my book. Once you list your topics or subjects to be featured in your book, you can start writing your book in the next chapter.

1. _____

2. _____

3. _____

4. _____

5. _____

6. _____

7. _____

8. _____

9. _____

10. _____

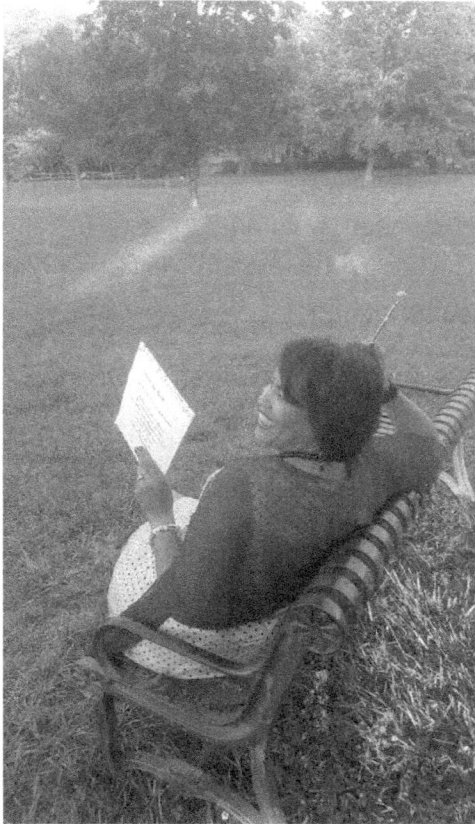

Chapter 2

Step Two – Unleash the Act of One Person Brainstorming

"I plan to write a book about my fitness journey and I don't know where to begin the process. What's the easiest way to get started?" –
Russell J. Guess

Now it's time to begin freestyle writing. If you don't know where to begin, start in the middle! Just start writing whatever comes to mind. I call it "One Person Brainstorming." When I began writing professionally 20 years ago, I would "brainstorm" a lot of subjects and topics for articles just to get me started. Then ... I could more easily zero in on the focus of my piece.

If you don't know where to begin, that's okay! It happens to me more often than you would think! That's okay! Just do as I do! Start in the middle! In other words, everything that is on your mind and heart, just start jotting it down.

Don't worry if it does not flow in the way that you would prefer. The important thing is that you are getting all of your ideas on paper. You can come back later to shape your writing into:

- Sentence form
- Paragraph form
- Essay form
- Article form
- And ultimately BOOK FORM!!!
- Feel free to add loose leaf paper if you run out of space here in the book. Whatever comes to mind, just write it down. Okay! Are you ready? Let's Get It Started!!!!

Chapter 3

Step Three – Employ the Basic Book Format

"I am working on two books. One is an inspirational book and the other is a coffee table book. How do I organize my thoughts to create my books?" -- Sharesa J. Alston

Having clarity of thought is paramount once you begin to shape your first book. In chapter two, you had the luxury of brainstorming. You were able to throw all of the paint against the wall to see what would stick! Now it's time to organize your book. It's really simpler than one might think. You can use this basic book format to get you started. And if you want to get fancy and add extras, Hey! Have at it! It's YOUR book!

Introduction
The introduction section can share your purpose or reason for writing your book. Additionally, I used it as an opportunity to give the reader a little background information about me. You can write your intro at the beginning if you like. Or you can wait until you've finished writing your book to complete the introduction. Either way is just fine. Just do what you feel.

Dedication Page
The dedication page is usually a page in which you express thanks to or give a shout-out to another person. Who are you dedicating your book to? My first book was dedicated to my husband, Tony, and my children – Antasha and Jay. I even added a family photo to further personalize it. Just think about who has been an immense blessing in your life. This book is dedicated to my beautiful mother who has been a wonderful inspiration.

About The Author
The about the author page is basically your biography or bio. Just share – on one page – what you want your readers to know about you.

Acknowledgements
The acknowledgements page is for people that have contributed to your book. These are people that helped you in the writing, researching, etc. of your book and you want to send a special shout-out to them. This is where you do it!

Resources
The resources page allows you to provide additional or supplemental information for your reader on your book's topic. It can include other books, websites and links.

Etcetera
If you like, you can add unique pages that are not typically included with books. I decided that I wanted to add additional info that I called Editors' Notes and Leslie's Library of Links. I respect the editors of my publications so much that I wanted them to have a quote in Leslie's Lane The Book! Leslie's Library of Links shared the links to all of the articles available online that I have written over the last 20 years.

Introduction

Dedication

About The Author

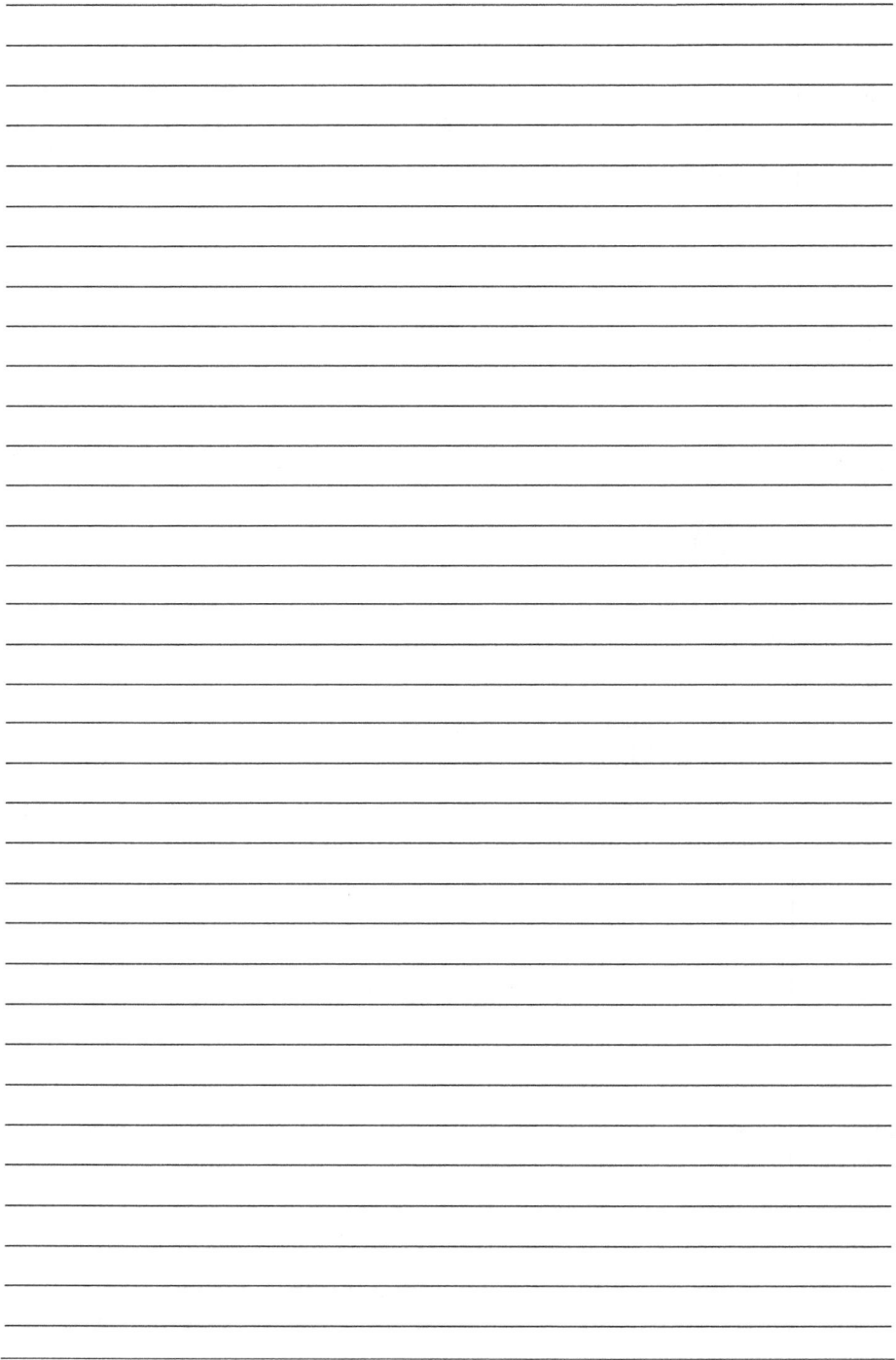

Acknowledgements

Resources

Etcetera

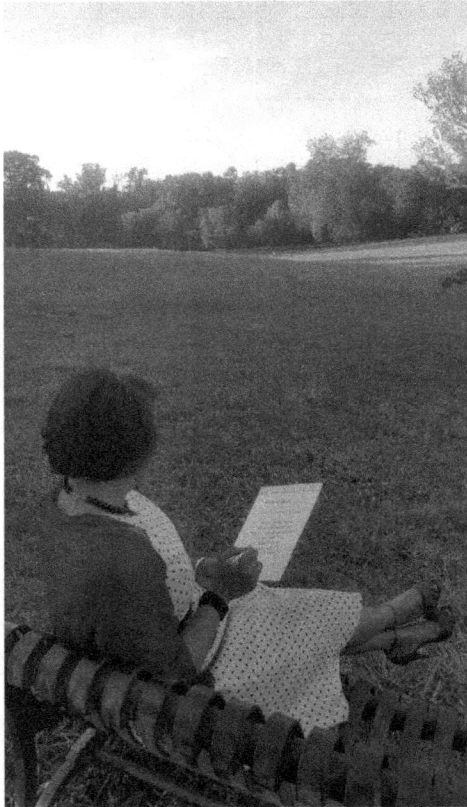

Chapter 4

Step Four - Create Your Timeline

"How do I stay focused and on schedule when writing my first book - especially since I have a full time job and have other obligations?" -- Liz Hudson

Creating a timeline is essential. This will assist you in staying focused, on track and meeting your deadlines. It's okay if you want to be aggressive in completing your manuscript. But you want to ensure that your timeline is practical and realistic. I've included my initial timeline for this book to give you reference. I've also included a fill in the blank one just for you!

TIMELINE

Weeks 1 & 2
February 1 - 14 –Brainstorming, Contact potential editors, Contact KDP re Questions and Begin Writing Book

BREAK TO FOCUS ON BOOK SIGNINGS AND FREELANCE WRITING PROJECTS

Weeks 3 & 4
March 6 - 18 – Writing Book, Taking Photos, Compiling Info, Getting Bio and Photos from Contributing Editors (300 word count bio and selfie with a high res image of at least 300 dpi)

BREAK TO FOCUS ON BOOK SIGNINGS AND FREELANCE WRITING PROJECTS

Week 5
April 1 – 5 – Send to Content Editors
April 6 – 7 – Changes by Author

Week 6
April 8 – 12 – First Round of Copy Editing
April 13 – 14 - Changes by Author

Week 7
April 15 - 19 – Second Round of Copy Editing
April 20 - 21 – Changes by Author

BREAK TO FOCUS ON BOOK SIGNINGS AND FREELANCE WRITING PROJECTS

Weeks 8 - 10
May 7 - 13 – Layout and Design by Graphic Designer
May 14 - 17 Edits by Author and Editors
May 18 – 21 Final Changes by Graphic Designer
May 22 – 27 Manuscript with Amazon's Self-Publishing Platform

Week 11
May 28 - 31 – Book Approved by Author and Ready for Sales

Week 12
June 1 – Book is Sold on Amazon and Book Launch Celebration is Scheduled

MANUSCRIPT TIMELINE FOR: _____

Book Title: _____

Week 1
Date: _____
Duties:

_____
_____
_____
_____
_____

Week 2

Date: _____
Duties:

_____
_____
_____
_____
_____

Week 3
Date: _____
Duties:

_____
_____
_____
_____
_____

Week 4

Date: _____

Duties:

_____

_____

_____

_____

Week 5

Date: _____

Duties:

_____

_____

_____

_____

Week 6

Date: _____

Duties:

_____

_____

_____

_____

Week 7

Date: _____

Duties:

_____

_____

_____

_____

Leslie's
Line

Chapter 5

Step Five - Write the Book!

How do I stay motivated to write and should I change my location in order to stay focused on my writing? – Walter Moore, Jr.

Get settled in a favorite room in your house or in a comfortable place of preference! You may want to go outside on your sun porch and enjoy the beauty of nature. When I started writing my first book, I wanted to get out of my every day environment. For four days, I went to the quiet, beautiful city of Serenbe on the outskirts of Atlanta and my creative juices just flowed. If you need to get away to the mountains, the beach, beautiful gardens or wherever, do so!

When you begin writing, you don't have to try to write brilliantly and profoundly. Just write - in plain language – precisely what you are thinking. Then go back to your manuscript and add all of the awesome adjectives you want to include to illustrate your point and vividly bring your book alive for the reader. You can write in the lines here or start typing on your computer. Whatever you do, know it's time to start writing! Just do what INSPIRES you!!!!!

_____
_____
_____
_____
_____
_____
_____
_____
_____
_____
_____
_____

Chapter 6

Step 6 - Enlist the Help of Others

"Once I have written my book, what is the process of moving forward with having it published? – Dr. Daphney F. Brooks

After you actually write the book and type your manuscript, you want to start the editing process. Think about those you want to help you. Although you can edit the book by yourself, I don't encourage it. I've been writing for years! But I can't edit myself! I'm thankful to my editors at *ESSENCE, Upscale, Black Enterprise, Dream Fearlessly*, etc. for catching my many typos!

For this book, I have asked my daughter Antasha, sisters Natalie and Sylathia, sorority sisters Deloris, Bernetta and Betty and my friend Michael Angelo Chester to serve as editors. Along with me, several of them are members of Berean Christian Church!

Ask family, friends, church members, sorority sisters, etc. if they would be willing to serve in different positions at no charge. Remember...... you are publishing the book for FREE! When the time comes around for those closest to you to write their book, you can return the favor! At a minimum, you want to have one copy editor.

The Content Editor checks the content of your book to ensure it is organized, makes sense to the reader and flows in a logical manner. Seek their candid feedback in making your book better.

The Copy Editor can also be called a proof reader. I suggest having two to three edits of your manuscript by at least two different people. These individuals help you ensure that your information is correct. They check for misspellings, errors, grammar and punctuation.

The Still Photography Editor is a position that I created for my book. This person is responsible for taking the photos to be used in the book and on the cover. The images should be high resolution with at least 300 dpi. Believe it or not, your smart phones can take great pics! (Just be sure to set it to HDR)

The Graphic Design & Layout Editor or Book Cover Editor takes your images and text and lays it out in a format of your choice. It can be as fancy, creative, simple or quirky as you like.

The Magnificent Seven Editors

1. Deloris Walker Birch – Copy and Line Editor
2. Michael Angelo Chester – Graphic Design/Book Cover Editor
3. Sylathia McCullough Johnson – Content, Copy and Line Editor
4. Dr. Bernetta Jones – Content, Copy and Line Editor
5. Natalie F. Reese – Copy and Line Editor
6. Antasha J. Royal – Still Photography Editor
7. Betty Pickett Stuckey – Copy and Line Editor

Select Your Book Team!

Name of The Copy Editor and Duties

_____
_____
_____
_____
_____

Name of The Content Editor and Duties

_____
_____
_____
_____
_____

_____

Name of The Still Photography Editor and Duties

_____

_____

_____

_____

_____

Name of The Graphic Design & Layout Editor and Duties

_____

_____

_____

_____

_____

Name of The Illustrator (Children's books, comics, etc.) and Duties

_____

_____

_____

_____

_____

Name of The _____ Editor and Duties

_____

_____

_____

_____

_____

Name of The _____ Editor and Duties

_____

_____

_____

_____

_____

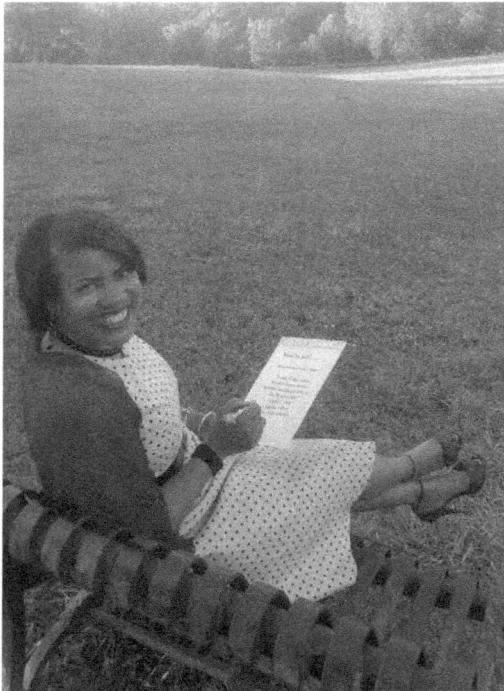

Chapter 7

Step Seven – Learn How to Self- Publish
With the Help of KDP

"If I decide to self-publish my upcoming children's book, how do I do so and what are the costs associated with it?" -- Tasia D. White

As you prepare to publish your book, you can consider whether it will be with a traditional publisher or through self-publishing. In the resources section, I've got links to the pros and cons of both. It would be wonderful to be accepted by a notable publisher! If you can, that will be amazing and you should most certainly go for it!

I've listed many of them, along with their contact information for you! However, if a publisher does not accept your manuscript, no worries! Don't let that stop you from following your dream of being an author! There is this whole new world of self-publishing! And quite frankly, I LOVE it! I have COMPLETE creative control of my Leslie's Lane series and that's the way that I prefer it!

5 Benefits of Self-Publishing Your Book

By Dr. Kerwin B. Lee

An Exclusive Article Written for This New Book!

Webster's Dictionary defines self-publishing as, "to publish a book using the author's own resources." There are a multitude of individuals who take on this endeavor on a weekly basis. The reason being is there are many benefits of self-publishing a book. This writing will share a few of them.

1. **You Control the Cost** - Self-publishing allows you, the writer, to determine what amount of money will be spent on the cover, design and marketing of the total project.

2. **You Reap the Total Harvest** - Self-publishing allows you to keep all of the financial return from your book. There is no split or percentage deal you have to work out with any outside party.

3. **You Determine Distribution** - Self -publishing allows you the freedom to move your product as fast or slow as you desire. The only timeline or constraint will be the one that you set.

4. **You Retain Rights** - Self-publishing allows you the opportunity to be the sole owner of your product. Through this means, there is never a need to worry about someone claiming your original work as their own.

5. **You Create Inventory** - Self-publishing will give the author peace about how many books to order. You won't have to worry about getting too many or not enough because you will be able to order based on your individual assessment.

These are just some of the advantages of self-publishing your own book. I advise you to research other options that may be available to you in order to accomplish your goal of being an author. Many individuals who have taken the route of traditional publishing can also be of help by sharing their experience from a different perspective. Regardless of which direction you choose, seek to make an informed decision.

Dr. Kerwin B. Lee, the Senior Pastor of Berean Christian Church in Stone Mountain, GA, is the author of four books!

Available on Amazon, They Are:

Winning the Battle Over Negative Emotions

Finding Joy in the Word of God – 52 Old Testament Bible Study Outlines

Feeding Your Soul with the Word of God – 52 New Testament Bible Study Outlines

The ABC's for Church Leaders – From A-Z: 26 Things You Should Do and Know About Ministry

Photo Credit: Courtesy of Julius Grimes, KreativTouch

After reading this valuable information from Dr. Lee, let's jump right into the final chapter! Time to learn how to self-publish for FREE with KDP! You may be self-publishing, but you are not in this thing alone. I have found KDP to be professional, reputable, kind, helpful, engaging and so much more!

They were willing to answer my questions – no matter how many or few! It didn't matter how simple or complex. They broke down everything in terminology and language that I could understand. They will certainly do the same for you! Anytime you have a question, just go to this link to contact them: https://kdp.amazon.com/contact-us. If needed, KDP offers limited phone support in English. Okay. Are you ready? Here we go!

Sign into Your Amazon Account
Go to the KDP.amazon.com website. If you are an Amazon shopper like me, you have an Amazon account. Utilize your login and password to sign in. If you don't have an Amazon account, no worries. Just click on the "sign up" key and you are well on your way to creating your new KDP account.

Create a New Title
There are two icons to begin the process of creating your new title. You can select Paperback or Kindle eBook to get started. For this book, we will navigate through the process of self-publishing your paperback.

Discover 4 Simple Paperback Details
1. Begin by selecting the primary language of your book. For me, it's English. Next, you will enter the book title for your manuscript. There is so much in a name. So, remember to select your title carefully. You can also include a subtitle. While it is optional, I think it's a really nice touch. Additional optional items include the series number and edition number.

2. **You will now enter the name of the primary author.** That's you! If there are additional authors, editors, illustrators, and other contributors, there is a section especially for that. This is certainly important for authors that have written children's books.

3. **You will give a description of your book.** This will be used as your manuscript is promoted through Amazon and other sales channels. In 4,000 characters or less, give an interesting, insightful description that draws in the reader.

4. **Publishing Rights, Key Words, and More.** You have two choices to select for publishing rights. You can select either I hold necessary publishing rights, or this is a public domain work. This is followed by your choosing up to seven key words to describe your new book as well as the categories and subcategories. Round out this section by checking the box if the book is to be in large print. Also check yes or no on the adult content. Press save and continue.

Get Your ISBN

The ISBN is required to publish a book. The ISBN is the International Standard Book Number used to identify each book. Click FREE KDP ISBN. If you would like to have your own name or business on the copyright page or would like to take your book and have it re-printed by another publisher, you can select use my own ISBN. There is an additional fee. Because I want to have entire creative control of my self-publishing, I pay to own my imprint or custom ISBN. As a KDP author, you can purchase your ISBN from Bowker at a discounted rate. Click: https://kdp.amazon.com/en_US/help/topic/G201834170.

Select Your Print Options

You can select your own interior. Your choices are black and white or color. The paper color choices are white or cream. However, for color books, the only option is white. Next, you will pick the trim size. In other words, this is the size of your book. My preference is 6 inches x 9 inches. This is the most popular size. Just be sure to ask if there are fees for varying page counts and ink types! For bleed settings, you'll select bleed or no bleed. That is, having your content to extend to the end of the page or allow for a small white margin. Now is time to select your cover finish. You can choose matte or glossy. I prefer glossy shiny things. With this book, my daughter Antasha took my cover photo and my friend Michael Angelo Chester created the design.

Upload Your New Manuscript and Book Cover!
You will upload your manuscript at this point. KDP encourages you to utilize a formatted PDF file. But no worries! They are really flexible. So, if your preference is for a DOC, DOCX, HTML, or RTF file, have at it! Go to this link to better understand how to submit your manuscript: https://kdp.amazon.com/en_US/help/topic/G201834190. To make formatting your book easier, go to this site for a KDP template: https://kdp.amazon.com/en_US/help/topic/G201834230. As for your book cover, you have two choices. Like me, you can upload a print-ready pdf cover that you already have. Or, you can select launch cover creator and design a cover with the assistance of KDP.

Preview the Book
Click book preview to check formatting of your manuscript. At this point, you will check to make certain that all of the information is uploaded as you like and that your title, ISBN, interior and cover information is correct. Once KDP makes certain the book meets submission requirements, they will email you within 72 hours with the next steps. Select save as draft or save and continue. (A point of clarification, KDP will review the book AFTER you have submitted it for publication. That will be after the following step.)

Decide on Distribution, Rights and Pricing
The standard distribution and certain types of expanded distribution are FREE. For no cost, your book can be distributed by Amazon in territories worldwide including North America, the United Kingdom, France, Germany, Italy, and Spain as well as other online retailers. After your book is uploaded in the "paperback content" section, printing costs are automatically calculated. In the "rights and pricing" section, you'll select territories in order to move on to the "pricing and

royalty" option. The minimum suggested list price will be in full view. The system will calculate your royalties and suggest pricing for Europe based on U. S. pricing.

Review

You can order what is known as a proof copy after pricing completion. This is an actual copy of the book which will give you an opportunity to see exactly what it will look like in print. Click the link to request the proof copy. This gives you an opportunity to make changes before the book is printed. Once you receive it, you can make your changes. If you don't need a proof copy, just click "Publish Your Paperback Book". Once KDP reviews and accepts it, you are now ready to sell it! It will take up to three days to be available on Amazon.

Sales and Marketing

Track your sales for FREE! They keep up with all of your sales! It's so cool to look at how many books I've sold! Talk about passive income! It is a great idea to check out the KDP forums to get FREE advice from your peers and others. You can wire into the KDP community and do research and get ideas. Check out this link: https://kdp.amazon.com/community/.

A Great Tip for You!

Check out this link to 12 simple steps in self-publishing on KDP. It provides supplemental information to further assist you with your first book! It's https://kdp.amazon.com/en_US/help/topic/G202187740. You will also learn how to format your eBook for Amazon Kindle.

ALL DONE!
CONGRATULATIONS ON
SELF-PUBLISHING YOUR BOOK!!!!!

About the Author

Leslie E. Royal is the Creator of Leslie's Lane – a Consumer Information Blog. It is designed to be informational, educational and inspirational. Her blog provides practical assistance in the area of jobs, discounts, free stuff, travel, scholarships, internships and a wealth of information individuals find helpful in their daily lives. Check it out at your leisure!

She is the author of ***How to Write and Self-Publish Your Book for FREE with Amazon's CreateSpace*** and ***Leslie's Lane The Book! Your One Stop Internet Resource Guide to Links for Jobs, Inspiration, Discounts, FREE Stuff, Scholarships, Travel & More!*** They are distributed by Amazon in more than 15 countries globally. Additionally, she has been a professional Freelance Writer for more than 20 years. She has written for many publications and online resources over her career.

Presently, she is a personal finance writer and international travel journalist for *ESSENCE, AAA Southern Traveler, UPSCALE* and *The Ashro Blog.* Her articles include cover features as well as parenting, business, consumer, Christian, history, travel, arts and high profile celebrity interviews. Leslie has been married to Tony Royal for 31 years.

Leslie is a member of Alpha Kappa Alpha Sorority, Inc. She is also a member of The University of Georgia Parents Association and Berean Christian Church in Stone Mountain, Georgia. She serves in the Deacons Ministry at her church. Because of their commitment to the community, the Royals have received many awards from churches, schools and other organizations. Leslie holds a Bachelor of Arts Degree in Journalism from Georgia State University as well as a Master of Arts Degree in Christian Studies and Master of Divinity from Luther Rice College and Seminary. She and Tony have two children - Antasha and Jay.

Check Out the Leslie's Lane Blog:
Jobs, FREE Stuff, Discounts, Resources & More!
https://leslieslane.wordpress.com/

Visit her website at www.LesliesLane.com

Follow Her @LesliesLane on Twitter and Instagram

https://www.facebook.com/LesliesLaneFREEStuff/

Distributed by Amazon in more than 15 countries globally and available on Amazon Kindle, order Leslie's Lane The Book!

Photo Credit: *In the "About the Author" image on page 72, the Age-Defying Makeover, Eyebrow Microblading, Mink Lashes and Mini Photo Shoot are Courtesy of Stephanie Janelle Bryant of Don Janelle Hair Salon in Decatur, GA. The cover page photo, back page photo and all other images of Leslie in this book are Courtesy of Antasha J. Royal, the Still Photography Editor. All Hairstyles are by Stephanie Janelle Bryant. Visit her website at:* ***www.jtcosmeticsandlashes.com***.

Resources

Example of a Press Kit
to Send to the Media to Promote Your Book

I would suggest that your press kit, media kit, press packet or media packet include five components – a press release, your bio, an About the Book page, a high resolution photo of yourself and high resolution photo of your book. Please find an example of my press release and about the book page below. Your bio can be the same info that you use on your About the Author page. Please check on my About the Author page. I use the very same info for my bio!

FOR IMMEDIATE RELEASE
Contact
Name:
Phone Number:
Email Address:

New Book Gives Inside Scoop on Jobs, FREE Stuff, Discount Travel, Scholarships and More!

ATLANTA (November, 14, 2016) - Leslie E. Royal, a personal finance journalist and travel writer of more than 20 years, has released her first manuscript entitled: *Leslie's Lane The Book!: Your One Stop Internet Resource Guide to Links for Jobs, Inspiration, Discounts, FREE Stuff, Scholarships, Travel & More!* The various chapters provide links to websites that offer countless dollars in savings and more than 500 job sites with innumerable job openings and opportunities for career advancement. Published by Amazon's CreateSpace, the book can be purchased for $14.95. For e-book lovers, the manuscript is also available on Kindle.

"I have always felt that anyone who wants a job ought to have one. I work hard to ensure that I provide information on getting gainful employment as well as information that consumers find helpful in their daily lives," says Leslie E. Royal, new author and creator of the

Leslie's Lane blog on WordPress. "Moreover, I love getting discounts and FREE stuff myself! Why pay full price when you can get products or services that are drastically discounted or at no cost at all?"

The book, a natural evolution of the Leslie's Lane blog, seeks to empower, inspire, educate and inform the readers about how they can simultaneously make and save money. As an added bonus, the manuscript offers invaluable perspectives from several top experts in their respective fields.

This book presents a great opportunity for individuals in the media to share valuable information with its readers, listeners, viewers, followers, family and friends. Here are a few ideas to consider!

- Interview Leslie for an article regarding one or more of the ten chapter topics – Jobs, FREE Stuff, Resources, FREE/Discount Travel, Financial Aid, Social Media, Follow Your Passion, Etc.
- Include *Leslie's Lane the Book!* in your Book Section, Roundup, Club, Den or Shelf
- Have a segment on buying *Leslie's Lane The Book!* as a stocking stuffer for Christmas.
- Why should Oprah have all the fun? Journalists can feature a holiday segment on The Blogger's, Editor's or Producer's Favorite Things and include *Leslie's Lane The Book!*
- Invite Leslie to get interactive on a Twitter chat or creatively engage on social media.
- Holding an undergrad degree in Journalism, Leslie's articles have appeared in *Upscale, FORTUNE, ESSENCE, Black Enterprise, Chron.com* and other international outlets. Ask her to write articles regarding saving money, getting a job or career advancement.
- Leslie has been excitedly and spiritedly covering topics in her book for more than 20 years! If you are having upcoming festivals, empowerment seminars, conferences and other sessions, it will be her pleasure to join you as an expert, moderator, facilitator or presenter.

Leslie is available for interviews in person, by phone or via email. Please find high resolution photos attached.

Leslie's Lane The Book!: *Your One Stop Internet Resource Guide to Links for Jobs, Inspiration, Discounts, FREE Stuff, Scholarships, Travel & More!*

By Leslie E. Royal

About the Book

Do you ever wonder where to start? With all of the tasks that need to be done and all of the information out there, it can feel impossible to know where to go for the advice you need.
Leslie's Lane The Book! is a continuation of the popular Leslie's Lane blog. The sole purpose of both is to provide you with all of the helpful info and tips you could ever need. The book covers everything from jobs and saving money to finding scholarships and free stuff on the Internet. It even targets specific issues like getting veterans' benefits and finding low-cost childcare.

Leslie is a thorough writer and researcher dedicated to giving you the best possible recommendations. Her knowledge of travel destinations is wide, and her network is even bigger. This book is full of opinions from experts and successful businesspeople. This inclusive book gives you the inside scoop on all things employment, money, and travel-related. It includes countless links to websites that have already been vetted by Leslie herself. With exhaustive knowledge and a level of care you can trust, Leslie provides all the tools to make your life easier and help you save money.

About the Author

Leslie E. Royal, the creator of Leslie's Lane consumer information blog, has been a professional freelance writer for over twenty years. She's written articles for many publications on a wide variety of topics, including consumer finance, careers, business and travel.

Leslie received a Bachelor's degree in Journalism from Georgia State University, as well as a Master's in Christian Studies and a Master of Divinity from Luther Rice Seminary and University. She is a member of Berean Christian Church in Stone Mountain, Georgia. She's a member of the Alpha Kappa Alpha Sorority, Inc. and her chapter's Forever Pink Foundation, Inc. Leslie is a member of The Authors Guild. She and her husband of 30 years, Tony, have two adult children, Antasha and Jay.

The blog Leslie's Lane is full of tips and practical assistance covering everything in daily life. Find Leslie online at her website www.LesliesLane.com or on Twitter and Instagram @LesliesLane.

Published by Amazon's KDP, the book can be purchased for $14.95. For e-book lovers, the manuscript is available on Kindle.

Resources

A Few Publishing Companies – Large and Small

If you sign on with a traditional publisher, you do not pay to publish your book. Plus, you might get paid in advance. However, if you self-publish with other publishing companies, there is a fee associated with editing, marketing, cover design, printing, distribution and other services.

Abbeville Family	www.abbeville.com
Abbeville Press	www.abbeville.com
Abdo Publishing	www.abdopublishing.com
Harry N. Abrams	www.abramsbooks.com
Acta Publications	www.actapublications.com
Adams Media	www.adamsmedia.com
Aladdin	www.simonandschuster.com
Avon Romance	www.avonromance.com
Baker Books	www.bakerpublishinggroup.com
Ballantine Bantam Dell	www.penguinrandomhouse.com
Black Heron Press	www.blackheronpress.com
Bloomberg Press	www.wiley.com
Blue Mountain Press	www.sps.com
Chosen Books	www.chosenbooks.com
Crown Publishing Group	www.crownpublishing.com
Dutton Children's Books	www.penguin.com
Four Way Books	www.fourwaybooks.com
Harlequin	www.harlequin.com
HarperCollins	www.harpercollins.com
John Wiley & Sons Inc	www.wiley.com
Kensington Publishing	www.kensingtonbooks.com
Merriam Press	www.merriam-press.com
Penguin Group USA	www.penguin.com
Random House Publishing	www.penguinrandomhouse.com
Rocky Mountain Books	www.rmbooks.com
Simon & Schuster	www.simonandschuster.com
Towering Publishing	www.towerpub.com
Tu Books	www.leeandlow.com/imprints/3

University of Arizona	www.uapress.arizona.edu
Viking	www.penguin.com
Zenith Press	www.zenithpress.com
Zumaya Publications, LLC	www.zumayapublications.com

Pros and Cons of Self-Publishing and Traditional Publishing – Check Out These Links!

http://www.huffingtonpost.com/brooke-warner/are-there-still-pros-to-t_b_5564672.html

https://www.amarketingexpert.com/the-benefits-of-self-publishing-vs-traditional-publishing/

http://www.thecreativepenn.com/self-publishing-vs-traditional/
http://bookmarketingtools.com/blog/the-pros-and-cons-of-self-publishing/#

http://www.writersdigest.com/online-editor/the-pros-and-cons-of-self-publishing-traditional-publishing

Leslie's Library of Links

Check Out a Few of Leslie's Litany of Articles Over the Past 23 Years!

FORTUNE.COM
http://fortune.com/2015/03/03/get-the-raise-you-deserve/

Dow Jones Newswires/The Wall Street Journal
https://blendle.com/i/wsj-com/fed-s-lockhart-downplays-fears-over-china-economy/bnl-wsj-20150923-SB11559093491392963941204581251202778291810
https://www.gfmag.com/topics/syndicate/35495566-feds-lockhart-downplays-fears-over-china-economy

Dream Fearlessly/Business Accelerator
https://www.dreamfearlessly.com/resource/share-your-expertise-and-boost-your-sales/
https://www.dreamfearlessly.com/resource/how-a-landing-page-converts-better-than-your-website/
https://www.dreamfearlessly.com/resource/how-to-reduce-costs-with-the-internet-of-things/
https://www.dreamfearlessly.com/resource/can-you-deduct-your-social-media-costs/
https://www.dreamfearlessly.com/resource/cutting-edge-marketing-strategies-to-attract-new-business/

ESSENCE and ESSENCE.com Articles Written by Leslie E. Royal
http://www.essence.com/authors/leslie-e-royal
http://www.essence.com/lifestyle/travel/road-trip-travel-guide
http://www.essence.com/lifestyle/travel/road-trip-travel-guide
http://www.essence.com/2016/08/29/fall-decorating-tips
http://www.essence.com/2016/07/08/essence-festivals-business-leadership-panel-offered-tips-getting-ahead-business
http://www.essence.com/2016/06/20/10-tips-owning-your-financial-future
http://www.essence.com/2016/01/15/sorority-power

http://www.essence.com/2015/12/17/5-unique-black-women-owned-venues-your-last-minute-holiday-soiree
http://www.essence.com/2015/12/03/shop-purpose-how-one-woman-managed-buyblack-year
http://www.essence.com/2015/11/24/cyber-sister-using-social-media-reach-your-niche-audience-holidays
http://www.essence.com/2015/11/15/it%E2%80%99s-sister-thing-importance-shopping-black-womens-businesses-season
http://www.essence.com/galleries/buyblack-essence-list-89-black-owned-businesses-shop-holidays
http://www.essence.com/2015/10/17/let%E2%80%99s-not-spend-much-money-christmas
http://www.essence.com/2014/11/14/shop-smart
http://www.essence.com/2014/04/13/how-gain-financial-freedom
http://www.essence.com/2015/02/23/sister-ceo-7-great-tips-starting-your-own-company-year http://www.essence.com/2015/02/23/5-great-ways-impress-your-boss-and-get-raise-you-deserve-2015
http://www.essence.com/2014/10/03/game-changers-power-list
http://www.essence.com/2015/01/01/join-2015-new-years-financial-revolution
http://www.essence.com/2014/10/02/rising-stars-michelle-bernard/
http://www.essence.com/2014/10/02/rising-stars-charlene-dance
http://www.essence.com/2014/11/28/broke-blessed-how-earn-multiple-streams-income
http://www.essence.com/2014/11/12/broke-blessed-getting-out-credit-card-debt
http://www.essence.com/2014/10/27/broke-blessed
http://www.essence.com/2014/09/18/5-smart-answers-tough-interview-questions
http://www.essence.com/2014/09/11/social-media-and-your-career-change
http://www.essence.com/2015/01/29/broke-blessed-how-manage-your-student-loan-debt
http://www.essence.com/2015/01/29/broke-blessed-increase-your-credit-score

Chron.com Articles Written by Leslie E. Royal
http://work.chron.com/build-oil-field-resume-27465.html

http://work.chron.com/revising-supervisor-do-27486.html
http://work.chron.com/become-christian-spiritual-retreat-director-28290.html
http://work.chron.com/copy-editor-career-outlook-26669.html

Black Enterprise Articles Written by Leslie E. Royal
http://www.blackenterprise.com/mag/recovering-from-bank-fraud/
http://www.blackenterprise.com/lifestyle/airline-passenger-rights-updated/
http://www.blackenterprise.com/mag/5-situations-when-it%E2%80%99s-ok-to-close-a-credit-card/
http://www.blackenterprise.com/mag/how-to-prepare-for-an-audit/
http://www.blackenterprise.com/lifestyle/become-an-empowered-patient/
http://www.blackenterprise.com/lifestyle/summer-travel-deals/
http://www.blackenterprise.com/lifestyle/green-credit-cards/
http://www.blackenterprise.com/mag/5-ways-to-reduce-debt/
http://www.blackenterprise.com/mag/save-money-on-healthcare-costs/
http://www.blackenterprise.com/mag/5-ways-to-build-your-budget/
http://www.blackenterprise.com/mag/choosing-the-right-tax-professional/
http://www.blackenterprise.com/mag/true-colors/
http://www.blackenterprise.com/mag/flying-the-passenger-friendly-skies/
http://www.blackenterprise.com/mag/its-a-family-reunion/
http://www.blackenterprise.com/mag/an-apple-a-day/
http://www.blackenterprise.com/mag/its-a-new-year/
http://www.blackenterprise.com/mag/its-a-family-affair-7/
http://www.blackenterprise.com/mag/the-rap-doctor/
http://www.blackenterprise.com/mag/i-apologize/
http://www.blackenterprise.com/mag/its-a-family-affair-2/
http://www.blackenterprise.com/mag/living-the-glamorous-life/
http://www.blackenterprise.com/mag/the-perpetual-world-of-change/
http://www.blackenterprise.com/mag/when-it-rains-it-pours/
http://www.blackenterprise.com/mag/going-once-going-twice-2/
http://www.blackenterprise.com/mag/the-mysterious-underwriters/
http://www.blackenterprise.com/mag/want-to-lower-your-auto-insurance/
http://www.blackenterprise.com/mag/in-too-deep/
http://www.blackenterprise.com/mag/the-clock-is-ticking/
http://www.blackenterprise.com/mag/the-doctor-will-e-mail-you-now/
http://www.blackenterprise.com/mag/its-in-the-mail/
http://www.blackenterprise.com/mag/vacation-research-made-easy/
http://www.blackenterprise.com/mag/the-rising-cost-of-medicine/
http://www.blackenterprise.com/mag/lost-in-translation/
http://www.blackenterprise.com/mag/all-the-right-moves/
http://www.blackenterprise.com/mag/unjust-clause/
http://www.blackenterprise.com/mag/total-recall-2/

http://www.blackenterprise.com/mag/homeowners-associations/
http://www.blackenterprise.com/mag/sour-auto-power/
http://www.blackenterprise.com/mag/whats-the-411-2/
http://www.blackenterprise.com/mag/settle-for-lesswith-the-irs/
http://www.blackenterprise.com/mag/high-speed-web-access/
http://www.blackenterprise.com/mag/forgive-us-our-debts-%e2%80%a6/
http://www.blackenterprise.com/mag/from-dream-to-reality/
http://www.blackenterprise.com/mag/first-time-visit-to-a-resale-shop/
http://www.blackenterprise.com/mag/fair-credit-reporting-act-tweaked-by-congress/
http://www.blackenterprise.com/mag/across-the-border/
http://www.blackenterprise.com/mag/get-used-to-it/
http://www.blackenterprise.com/mag/legal-ease/
http://www.blackenterprise.com/mag/looting-luggage/
http://www.blackenterprise.com/mag/im-sorry-just-wont-do/
http://www.blackenterprise.com/mag/no-saving-grace/
http://www.blackenterprise.com/mag/home-free/
http://www.blackenterprise.com/mag/tightening-your-belt/
http://www.blackenterprise.com/mag/looks-like-a-bargain/
http://www.blackenterprise.com/mag/heated-about-your-gas-bill/
http://www.blackenterprise.com/mag/not-for-sale/
http://www.blackenterprise.com/mag/art-aids-africa/
http://www.blackenterprise.com/mag/creditors-in-your-closet/
http://www.blackenterprise.com/mag/whats-the-411/
http://www.blackenterprise.com/mag/creepin-credit-errors/
http://www.blackenterprise.com/mag/housing-bias-bust/
http://www.blackenterprise.com/mag/when-diamonds-arent-forever/
http://www.blackenterprise.com/mag/all-inclusive-trips/
http://www.blackenterprise.com/mag/happy-kwanzaa/
http://www.blackenterprise.com/mag/top-10-reasons-to-dump-your-bank/
http://www.blackenterprise.com/mag/smart-credit-card-use/
http://www.blackenterprise.com/mag/save-time-and-money-on-the-net/
http://www.blackenterprise.com/mag/online-shoppers-beware/
http://www.blackenterprise.com/mag/consumer-information-catalog/
http://www.blackenterprise.com/mag/debt-free-is-the-way-to-be/
http://www.blackenterprise.com/mag/free-online-surfing/
http://www.blackenterprise.com/mag/email-travel-savings/
http://www.blackenterprise.com/mag/cut-your-mortgage-cost/
http://www.blackenterprise.com/mag/hip-hop-on-top/

Acknowledgement Of The Magnificent 7

The Magnificent Seven Editors

Deloris Walker Birch
Copy and Line Editor

Michael Angelo Chester
Graphic Design/Book Cover Editor

Sylathia McCullough Johnson
Content, Copy and Line Editor

Dr. Bernetta Jones
Content, Copy and Line Editor

Natalie F. Reese
Copy and Line Editor

Antasha J. Royal
Still Photography Editor

Betty Pickett Stuckey
Copy and Line Editor

Acknowledgements
Deloris Walker Birch – Copy and Line Editor

Deloris Walker Birch was born in the Mississippi Delta, commonly called the "Cotton Capital of the World," and home of the blues. She acquired her Bachelor of Arts degree in English/Journalism with honors at Tougaloo College, Tougaloo, Mississippi.

Deloris is presently an advocate for people with disabilities and serves high school seniors with learning disabilities in the Atlanta Public Schools where she provides job readiness training skills transitioning them from *school to work.*

Deloris is an active member of Greenforest Community Baptist Church, NAACP, and Alpha Kappa Alpha Sorority, Incorporated, Lambda Epsilon Omega Chapter, DeKalb County, GA where she serves in many capacities. She enjoys traveling, writing poetry, singing, line dancing, networking, creating synergy, and implementing new ideas to make a difference in the lives she touch.

Deloris's *mantra* is, "Whatever is worth doing at all is worth doing well." She is happily married to Barnett Birch and has two lovely daughters, Bernadette and Morgan. Deloris also has a grand dog named Anderson who is dear to her heart. She resides in Lithonia, Georgia.

Photo Credit: Taken by AKA Sorority Sister, Willieyour Arnold

Acknowledgements
Michael Angelo Chester – Graphic Design Cover Editor

Born in Columbus, Georgia and raised in Detroit, Michigan, Michael is a "visualist" whose career spans several decades. His exceptional work includes visual media, fine art, graphic art, still photography and film/video. Michael obtained his degree in graphic arts from The Computer Arts Institute in San Francisco.

He has designed CD covers, books, logos, and magazine ads for numerous clients. He created the cover image and interior graphics as well as served as the photographer for many of the images for Leslie's first manual entitled: *Leslie's Lane The Book! Your One Stop Internet Resource Guide to Links for Jobs, Inspiration, Discounts, FREE Stuff, Scholarships, Travel & More!*

Photo Credit: Courtesy of Michael Angelo Chester

Acknowledgements
Dr. Bernetta Jones – Content, Copy and Line Editor

Dr. Bernetta Jones is an energetic and motivating educator who believes that all children can learn "If we begin where the child is and work vigorously to take him where he needs to be". Having more than 25 years of experience at the elementary, middle, and high school levels, Bernetta is known for captivating and motivating audiences and students, when she speaks.

Prior to beginning her fantastic voyage as an educator, Bernetta was commissioned as a United States Army Officer through ROTC at Fort Valley State University. Trained as an Intelligence Officer, she served as a Platoon Leader in Desert Storm.

Bernetta earned a Bachelor of Science in Education from Fort Valley State University. She earned graduate degrees in Ed Leadership and Middle Grades from Valdosta State University, and completed her doctoral studies in Ed Leadership at Argosy University, Sarasota, Florida. Bernetta is a life member of Alpha Kappa Alpha Sorority, Inc. She is a member of its Lambda Epsilon Omega Chapter. Bernetta enjoys spending quality time with her beautiful daughter, Taylor, and with family members and friends. She also enjoys baking, reading, and traveling.

Photo Credit: Victor Powell, Powell Photography, Chicago, IL

Acknowledgements
Sylathia McCullough Johnson – Content, Copy and Line Editor

Sylathia McCullough Johnson was born in Little Rock, Arkansas. She is the second oldest of five siblings. She is married to Edward F. Johnson and they have one daughter, Ernestine (aka Tina).

She is employed by Williams, Maxheimer & Associates, LLC, a real estate appraisal company in Savannah, GA, where she has held the position of Office Manager for over 25 years. She is a member of St. Luke Baptist Church. She has an Associate's Degree in Accounting from Everest University.

Sylathia also received a certificate in Clerical Training from Riley Training Institute in 1991. She held the highest GPA (99.0) in her graduating class. She enjoys working with computers learning new applications and repairing them for work, family, and friends.

She is a member of the Savannah High School Mass Alumni Association where she holds the position of Secretary. She enjoys being a member of this organization because their main goals are to support the students, organizations, and faculty and staff at Savannah High School. Sylathia also enjoys spending time with her family and going on cruises with her husband.

Photo Credit: Taken by her hubby, Ed, on deck of cruise to Belize

Acknowledgements
Natalie F. Reese – Copy and Line Editor

     Natalie Reese resides in Atlanta Georgia. An alumnus of University of Phoenix, she has an Associate of Arts Degree in Foundations of Business. Having 16 years of management experience, she has worked with great companies like Chick-fil-A and Payless Shoes.

     Natalie has a passionate creative flair for cooking which grows each time someone experiences her cuisines. Some of her family and friend's favorite dishes that she prepares are savannah red rice, crab & cream cheese stuff salmon, collard greens and mac & cheese.

     She is best known for her delectable sweet potato pie. Her family says it is DIVINE! She is a member of 1st & 10 football group originated out of Savannah Georgia created on social media app Facebook. This group engages year-round on Facebook, on an annual cruise, at the annual meet and greet weekend, at several charity fund raisers, and on game days.

     A Green Bay Packers fan, she likes to go to football games and watch them on television. Natalie is the mother of three children – Jesse, Tommy, and LeTonya. She is the grandmother of two grandchildren – Gabrielle Elizabeth and Jesse Robert.

Photo Credit: Selfie by Natalie

Acknowledgements
Antasha J. Royal – Still Photography Editor

Antasha Royal was born in Atlanta, Georgia to Tony and Leslie E. Royal and is the elder of two siblings. Antasha is a dynamic and driven individual who truly lives by the motto "Live, laugh, love." She believes in going out and enjoying life by living it to the fullest, trying new things, and doing what she loves.

A Georgia girl, born and bred, she is a graduate of the University of Georgia, where she double majored in Psychology and Sociology. Antasha has over thirteen years of educational and professional experience, primarily as a manager at Chick-fil-A. It was there that she honed skills in marketing, talent acquisition and sales building.

Although, rewarding, she soon found herself drawn to the field of aviation. Her passion for people and travel is currently fueled by her career as a full-time Atlanta based flight attendant. Although she loves to travel and has been to several different countries, she loves to lounge at home with a good book and either a glass of wine or coffee. Due to her limited cooking skills, her favorite meal of the day is breakfast. Her most favorite food of all time is chocolate (which she believes deserves its own food group).

Antasha is also the creator of the Nomadic Flight Attendant Blog where she writes about her many adventures travelling! You can follow her on Facebook, Instagram, and Twitter!

Photo Credit: Selfie by Antasha

Acknowledgements
Betty Pickett Stuckey – Copy and Line Editor

Betty P. Stuckey is a native Texan, who has resided in Lithonia, GA (metro Atlanta) for 25+ years. She has a Master's of Business Administration Degree from Georgia State University and a Bachelor's of Business Administration Degree in Accounting from the University of Houston.

Betty has over 40 years of experience in financial services and accounting. She retired from a financial services company in 2016 after working 30 years in various management positions, where she received several leadership awards for excellence.

Betty was the President of Lambda Epsilon Omega Chapter of Alpha Kappa Alpha, Sorority, Incorporated® from 2014 – 2017 serving the community of DeKalb County, GA. She also served as Vice President for the Forever Pink Foundation, Incorporated, and chairman of various committees for Lambda Epsilon Omega Foundation, Incorporated. Betty volunteers with many other community service organizations.

Betty and her husband of over 40 years, Samuel A. Stuckey enjoy spending time with their daughter and son-in-law, Krystal and Aubrey Brooks.

Photo Credit: Courtesy of Prim and Proper Photography

After Seven

More Acknowledgments

My Hubby – Tony Royal *AND* My Son – Jay Royal

P. Nigel Killikelly – Graphic Design Consultant
Krystal Stuckey Brooks – Graphic Design Consultant
Lady Anne Williams-Aplin * Andrea Aplin-Little (Shaye)
Stephanie Janelle Bryant * Donna London
Bryson Jones * Lisa Kirk * Neva Jones * LeTonya Reese

Dr. Kerwin B. Lee and Lady Yolanda T. Lee
and The Berean Christian Church Family

Alpha Kappa Alpha Sorority, Inc.
Lambda Epsilon Omega Chapter and Other Members

The International Media Ladies
Annita Stokes Thomas, Janet McCloud Montgomery, Rashan Ali, Brenda
O'neale, Antasha J. Royal, Valerie Morgan, Mackenzie Morgan, Twanda
Black, Michelle Gipson, Malika Bowling, Dawn Richards, Lorraine
Ferguson and Sheiresa Ngo

Thanks for Supporting My Family, Writing and Leslie's Lane!
Debbie Geiger and the Geiger Team, The Chick-fil-A Family, Tim
Tassopoulos, Marsha Middleton, Dr. Cheryl D. Dozier, Dr. Benson
Karanja, Kimberly Wigley, Sheryl Nance-Nash, Dr. Tan Goodjoines
Marilla, Tim Pearson, Alzena Anderson, Dr. Patti Copenny Reed, Helen
Guess Jones, Alzena Anderson, Joia Ellis-Dinkins, Sybil Jones, Cheryl
Cross, Dr. Linda Williams Smith, Cynthia Calvert, Terry Sprunger,
Patrick T. Cooper, Kathy Mitchell, Jennifer Parker, Cheryl Collins-
Coulton, Beth McKenna, Dennis Stokely and Beth Eastham

ABOVE ALL, I AM THANKFUL TO MY CREATOR!

www.ingramcontent.com/pod-product-compliance
Lightning Source LLC
Chambersburg PA
CBHW031521040426
42445CB00009B/331

* 9 7 8 1 7 3 2 9 1 9 1 0 5 *